CaReeR moves

FOR TEACHERS
AND OTHER PROFESSIONALS

*Strategies for
a Successful Job Change*

Geraldine Hogan

VITAL
PUBLISHING, INC.

Career Moves for Teachers and Other Professionals:
Strategies for a Successful Job Change

Copyright © 2019 Geraldine Hogan.

All rights reserved. No part of this book may be used or reproduced in any manner whatsoever — except in the case of brief quotations embodied in articles and reviews — without written permission of the publisher. For information contact Vital Publishing, Inc. gbh@geraldinehogan.com

Cover design by: Layne Mitchelle, Layne Creative Services

Interior design by: Patrizia Sceppa, Inc.

Printed in the United States of America.

Library of Congress Control Number: 2019905953

ISBN

978-1-7331278-0-6 (paperback)

978-1-7331278-1-3 (hardback)

978-1-7331278-2-0 (Ebook/Kindle)

This book is dedicated to my parents, the late John and Cordelia Brown. Their guidance and unconditional love will always be with me. And to my husband, Steve. Thank you for your love, patience, and encouragement. You are a continual source of inspiration.

CONTENTS

INTRODUCTION 3

Chapter One
The Power of YOUR THINKING 13

Chapter Two
Make a DECISION TO CHANGE 29

Chapter Three
FEAR 41

Chapter Four
Complacency: A SILENT KILLER 53

Chapter Five
Set GOALS 61

Chapter Six
Create a PLAN 73

Chapter Seven
Take ACTION 83

Chapter Eight
Unforeseen OBSTACLES 93

A Few Last WORDS 100

About the AUTHOR 103

ACKNOWLEDGMENTS 105

Notes and BIBLIOGRAPHY 106

> "If today were the last day of your life, would you want to do what you're about to do today?"
>
> Steve Jobs

INTRODUCTION

Teaching is one of the noblest of all professions.

It's not just a job. It's not just a career. It's a calling. So what happens when you no longer want to teach and begin to wonder whether your love for the profession ever existed?

My friend Carolyn taught high school English for more than four decades. She loved teaching and sharing her passion for writing with her students. Although the world needs more Carolyns, you may not be one of them.

You may be more like Anna. Anna is in her mid-twenties and has been teaching for approximately two years. The job isn't what she expected. Although she's ashamed to admit it, she hates teaching. She tells herself that, with more experience, the job will get easier. But deep in her heart she knows that she's in the wrong profession.

Maybe you've enjoyed teaching for many years but feel that it's time for a change. You remember with fondness a time when you felt as if you were called to teach. You worked well with students and coworkers. You felt supported by school administrators and had great relationships with your students' parents. But somewhere along the way you lost your zeal. The demands of student testing and increased responsibilities unrelated to teaching left little room for creativity. At some point—you're not sure when—you started to dread coming to work. Although frustrated with your current job, you feel that a career change at this stage of your life isn't possible.

The Beginning and End of MY TEACHING CAREER

I wanted to be a teacher ever since I was a little girl. Every day, upon returning from school, I gathered my dolls around me, and I taught. When I learned to add, I taught my dolls addition. When I learned to subtract, I taught subtraction. My favorite teaching activity was retelling the stories read by my teacher to my mannequin students. Throughout elementary school, pretending to be a teacher was my favorite play activity. If I wasn't pretending to teach my dolls, I taught my younger brother or my next-door neighbor. Sometimes I instructed imaginary students. There wasn't any doubt in my mind that I would grow up to become a teacher.

> *"I WANTED to be a teacher ever since I was a LITTLE GIRL."*

Although I outgrew playing with dolls and pretending to be a teacher, my desire to teach continued. The summer after completing eleventh grade, I had the opportunity to work as a student assistant at an elementary school. This job required me to tutor students in reading and math. I looked forward to going to work every day.

My passion for teaching continued through undergraduate and graduate school. After receiving my Master of Education degree, I began my career as an elementary school teacher in Gainesville, Florida. I thought that I would teach until retirement.

After teaching for many years I started to notice that things had changed since I started my career. I couldn't tell if I had changed or if the students were different. I think it was a little of both. One day, after I congratulated the head custodian at my school on his upcoming retirement, he asked how many more years I needed to work before I could retire. After I advised him that I had not yet considered retirement, I began calculating quietly in my mind. Based on my calculation, it would be approximately thirty years before I could retire. That seemed like a very, very long time. I knew teachers who seemed ready to quit, and they were younger than I would be by retirement age.

Although I wasn't completely ready for a career change at the time, I began to consider other career options. I read books and articles on alternative careers. I asked friends about the specific responsibilities of their jobs and what they did or didn't enjoy about their work. While considering the possibility of a new career I was summoned to jury duty and selected to serve for a DUI trial. During the trial I imagined myself standing before the jury as an attorney. Watching the attorneys deliver their opening and closing statements reminded me of my fondness for storytelling.

The Big LEAP

The idea of becoming an attorney stayed in my mind long after my service as a juror ended. A year later, I took a course to prepare myself for the Law School Admissions Test. I didn't make the decision to apply to law school with boldness and confidence. It had been at least a decade since I completed graduate school, and I doubted my ability to meet the demands of a law school curriculum. Additionally, I had no idea how I could pay for law school and continue to meet my other financial obligations.

That was my husband's biggest and perhaps only concern with my plan to pursue a new career. I decided not to focus on the details of attending law school before receiving an acceptance letter.

I won't discuss the physical, mental, and emotional demands of earning a law degree, but my husband and I figured out how to afford it and, at age forty, I graduated from the University of Florida College of Law.

During my last semester of law school, I was offered a job working as a prosecutor for the Miami-Dade State Attorney's Office. After moving to Miami, I worked as an attorney for several years, first as a prosecutor and later as a workers' compensation attorney. I was working for the City of Miami, litigating workers' compensation claims, when I decided to apply for a judicial appointment.

Moving FORWARD

In Florida, workers' compensation judges are appointed by the governor. I didn't receive an appointment the first time I applied. After this unsuccessful attempt, a coworker gave me some useful advice. I don't recall her exact words, but it was something like this: "The process

Geraldine Hogan

Pursue

Employ specific

strategies in

order to reach a

desired goal.

of receiving a judicial appointment is a game. You must know the rules and you must know the players."

I can't say that I ever learned the rules or identified the players. But a few years later another position opened in the Fort Lauderdale District Office, and I decided to apply. This time I sought the advice of people who knew the game, the rules, and the players, and with the advice and help of so many people, I had the opportunity to serve the citizens of the State of Florida as a judge of compensation claims for twelve years.

It's been nearly thirty years since I had that conversation with the head custodian at my school. I've now retired from my judicial position and started a business as a private mediator. In that role, I help litigants resolve cases informally, without judicial intervention. My goal is to spend as much time as I can doing work that I enjoy.

So, what about you? Have you thought about making a career change, but not taken the first step? Perhaps you've taken the first step but could benefit from some encouraging words to keep the momentum going. In this book, I share ideas that can help you make a major—

or minor—career move, if you know that it is time for you to do so.

"You are TODAY where your thoughts have brought you; you will be TOMORROW where your thoughts take you."

James Allen

Chapter One
The Power of YOUR THINKING

Can you imagine getting out of bed in the morning, full of energy and looking forward to starting your work day?

And this day of excitement did not begin when you woke up. It began with a thought; maybe a thought planted in your mind days, months, or even years ago. Perhaps one of life's greatest lessons is that we can completely alter our lives by altering the thoughts that we hold in our minds.

Norman Vincent Peale, author of *The Power of Positive Thinking*, advises that we can think our way to failure and unhappiness, but we can also think our way to success and happiness. He further notes that the world in which we live is not primarily determined by outward conditions and circumstances but instead by the thoughts that habitually occupy our minds.[1] But where do those thoughts come from? Our current thoughts about our world and how our lives should be are primarily based on our past experiences, our relationships, and the information we consume. However, as you will see in the following examples, we cannot allow past experiences, relationships, or information received to limit our thinking about how our lives should be and what we can accomplish.

Past EXPERIENCES

We can't undo our past. However, we can learn from previous experiences and decide to make the rest of our lives as good as possible. This precept is demonstrated by the life of Johnnetta McSwain. In her book *Rising Above the Scars*, McSwain recounts a childhood of severe sexual, physical, and emotional abuse.[2] Although she dropped out of high school in the eleventh grade, she later received a GED, continued her education, and became the first person in her family to graduate from college. She later helped to establish and implement an intervention program designed to help women overcome the consequences of tragic experiences. Johnnetta realized that she had absolutely no control over her childhood, but she had one hundred percent control over her adulthood. She reminds us to never allow horrific experiences from the past to limit our thinking about what we can accomplish in the future.

Past experiences also include ideas placed in our minds by people we hold in high esteem, like our parents and teachers. I grew up in a small town in Alabama. I still recall the day my ninth-grade science teacher told the class that our school district ranked among the lowest in the state and that the schools in Alabama ranked among the lowest in the country. I'm not sure why he felt compelled to provide us with this demoralizing information. Maybe it was his way of motivating us to work hard in order to pass his class. However, I felt he was informing us that we were receiving an inferior education compared to students attending schools in the rest of the country.

I didn't think too much about my teacher's comments until my first year of college. One day I met several students from New Jersey. While we were introducing ourselves and talking about where we grew up, my mind flashed back to the comments of my ninth-grade science teacher. I instantly felt academically inferior, though our conversation had nothing to do with academics. Comments made by an insensitive teacher my first year of high school were imbedded in my mind and four years later caused me to doubt my ability to receive a post-secondary degree. Although I had some struggles during my freshman year, I eventually adjusted to college life and developed the discipline required to graduate with honors. I could not allow a negative message from my past to limit my thinking about what I could accomplish.

RELATIONSHIPS

The fact that our thoughts are influenced by others can obviously work to our benefit or detriment. Many of us spend time with friends, coworkers, family members, and others by happenstance. We may never consider how our relationships influence our thoughts, our actions, and our lives. Have you ever found yourself in a meeting or breakroom at work engaged in a conversation where everyone involved is complaining about the boss, another coworker, or negative aspects of the work environment? The next time you find yourself in that, or a similar situation, ask yourself if the conversation positively or negatively influences your attitude about the person or circumstances discussed.

In his book *The Success Principles*, author Jack Canfield recalls his first year teaching in a Chicago high school.[3] He stopped spending time in the teachers' lounge, which he dubbed the "Ain't It Awful Club," because of the negative energy

"... ask yourself if the conversation POSITIVELY or negatively influences your ATTITUDE about the person or circumstances discussed."

created by the complaints and negative comments of his fellow teachers. He began spending time with positive like-minded colleagues, undaunted by the challenges of the profession. These coworkers shared ideas that enhanced the quality of his teaching. Time spent with this group of teachers contributed to his success and resulted in his selection by the students as teacher of the year. Spending time with coworkers who were positive about their work not only helped Canfield to maintain a positive attitude, but also enhanced the quality of his job performance.

When I decided to change careers in my mid-thirties, I spent a lot of time talking with a friend from undergraduate school. She was also preparing to expand her career options by continuing her education. I lived in Florida and she lived in New York, so we didn't see each other, but spoke often by phone. We encouraged each other to move out of our comfort zones and start the journey toward reaching the next career goal. Whenever I spoke with her, I ended the conversation with a positive attitude and motivated to face whatever challenges lay ahead of me.

Another friend and I applied to law school around the same time. We were close in age and were both attempting to start a new career. Although she encouraged me to move forward with my plan to become an attorney, I soon learned that her husband felt both our efforts to pursue a legal career were a waste of time and money. We lived in the same city and my husband and I considered them friends. Though my friend started law school, she never finished. I can't blame her husband for the unaccomplished goal, but her situation reminds me that the people who are the closest to us can foster our most negative thoughts and those negative thoughts may yield negative results. This is one reason why our greatest tool for enhancing the quality of our thinking may be the information we consume.

INFORMATION We CONSUME

Even without the support of family and friends, we have unlimited access to information that can positively influence our thoughts and actions. When I first considered leaving my job as a teacher to pursue a legal career, computer access to information was somewhat limited compared to what it is today. I still recall the first personal development book I ever read. It was a hardcover edition of a motivational classic, *See You at the Top* by Zig Ziglar. Today we're not limited to purchasing books from a bookstore or checking them out from a library. We have unlimited access to electronic books, in audio and print formats. Access to online articles, podcasts, and YouTube videos is also unlimited and available within a matter of seconds without leaving the comfort of home.

If you're new to personal development literature, I recommend the following three books as a start: *How to Win Friends and Influence People* by Dale Carnegie; *The Power of Positive Thinking* by Norman Vincent Peale; and *Think and Grow Rich* by Napoleon Hill. Although these books were written decades ago, they're classics, and the ideas discussed are as relevant today as they ever were. They are also available in updated editions and audio recordings. An internet search of "personal growth books" will include recently published books as well as other classics. Reading this type of literature may influence your thoughts and encourage you to set and reach goals that can enhance the quality of your professional and personal life.

Author and speaker Charlie "Tremendous" Jones asserted, "You are the same today as you'll be in five years except for two things, the people you meet and the books you read."[4] Five years before starting law school, I was still teaching. Less than five years after I began, I had completed law school, completed the licensing exams, and found work as a licensed attorney. Several books, not counting the required reading for my classes, helped me through this journey.

I'm reminded of an injury I sustained during my first year of law school. I suffered a severe ankle sprain rushing to turn in a paper by the deadline. I had been up all night and half the day completing the final draft. Sitting in the emergency room looking at my ankle, which was swollen to three times its normal size, I thought for sure it was broken. I was exhausted from lack of sleep and in excruciating pain. I tried to imagine getting to classes on crutches carrying a backpack filled with books, each weighing approximately five pounds. Rather than giving in to the urge to break down and cry uncontrollably, I thought of something that I read in Ziglar's *See You at the Top*. It was a story about a young man who was diagnosed with cerebral palsy as an infant. With the help of his parents he developed the physical capacity to live a relatively normal life, despite the predictions of several doctors, who suggested that his parents place him in an institution. His ability to walk, swim, and ride a bicycle were the result of an extremely demanding regimen of physical exercises performed every day of his life.[5]

A brief reflection on this man's life changed my thoughts from feeling totally helpless to thinking of my current situation as a mere inconvenience. Just recalling something that I had previously read changed my state of mind in a matter of seconds. What we read and listen to can provide a reservoir of encouraging information to draw from to positively alter our thinking in a relatively short period of time.

We cannot undo past experiences, and our family, friends, and coworkers may not have the desire or ability to help us develop and maintain a positive mindset. But we can inundate our minds with positive and encouraging information provided by the most motivational and inspirational authors who ever lived.

Even if you are considering a career move, do your best to maintain a positive attitude about your current job. Avoid negative conversations with disgruntled coworkers who may negatively influence your thoughts. If your thoughts are negative, your actions may be also. In order to move forward in your current career or to build

Positive

The required

mindset needed

in order to reach a

desired goal.

a new one, it's imperative that you maintain a positive attitude. And a positive attitude is a direct result of your thinking.

Life experiences, relationships, and the information we consume will influence our thoughts, and our thoughts will determine the trajectory of our lives.

QUESTIONS

1 What past experiences have shaped your journey to date? Are there obstacles you still must overcome?

2 Are the people with whom you spend the most time helping you to develop and maintain a positive attitude regarding your professional and personal goals?

3 Are the books, articles, blogs, YouTube recordings, television programs, and podcasts that you read, watch, and listen to helping you to develop and maintain a positive attitude regarding your professional and personal goals?

Career Moves for Teachers and Other Professionals

Think about it.

A positive attitude will help you develop the proper perspective on making a career change. You may find that, after much thought, where you are is where you want to stay. Or you may find that, though there are many positive aspects of your current position, it's time for a change.

> "If you don't like how things are, change it! You're not a tree."
>
> Jim Rohn

Chapter Two
Make a
DECISION TO CHANGE

For some individuals, the thought of change is paralyzing.

If the idea of a career move causes you to experience major anxiety, consider getting professional help or talking with someone you trust about your feelings. However, resist the urge to reveal your plans to everyone you know. Friends and family members may not understand why you are contemplating a career move and may discourage you by voicing their unsolicited opinions. This is especially true if a new career goal appears inconsistent with your previous education, training, and work history. Some may feel that you are throwing away many years of education and experience with no guarantee of success in your new pursuit. You will probably have several moments of self-doubt, so you will not want additional discouragement from others.

Accept feelings of apprehension as normal. However, do not allow doubts and fears to prevent you from moving forward. Remember the words of William Shakespeare in *Measure for*

Measure: "Our doubts are traitors, and makes us lose the good we oft might win, by fearing to attempt."[6] Commit to making a change and then move forward. We'll discuss fear later.

After you commit to making a change, decide on the career or job that you would like to pursue, if you have not done so already. You don't have to figure out all the details at this point. Just make sure that your decision is based on what you want and not on a desire to please or impress someone else.

Decide What YOU WANT

The first step in making a change in any area of life is to decide what you want. I know several teachers that decided to make a career move. Most of them received an additional degree or certification in educational leadership and pursued employment opportunities as an assistant principal, principal, or superintendent of a public school district. If your desire is to pursue a career in leadership, I strongly encourage you to pursue that goal. Just make sure that your decision is based on what you want and not based on what someone else believes you should do.

Serving as a juror for a criminal trial was the catalyst for my legal career. However, when I

Decide

Create in your

mind a firm

choice about

what you would

like to achieve or

accomplish.

started law school, I thought it best to pursue a career either in education law or some area of law that addressed the needs of children. Without consciously realizing it, I made this decision based on what I thought would make sense to career counselors, family members, and friends. After learning more about education law, I did not believe that this was an area of law that I wanted to pursue.

For many of us who graduated from high school and continued our education, we have at least one thing in common. We know how to follow rules and work within established boundaries. Without thinking about it, many—if not most—of us developed the habit of pleasing others. This trait served us well in completing our educational goals. However, the habit of pleasing others may prevent us from pleasing ourselves and pursuing work that we enjoy.

DON'T KNOW What You Want?

I recently spoke with a friend who is currently teaching first grade. Like me, she wanted to teach from the time she was a child and has worked as a teacher for many years. She stated that her passion for teaching is gone, but she doesn't know what she wants to do. Over the years I've talked with many individuals who

"Without thinking about it, many—if not most—of us developed the HABIT of PLEASING OTHERS."

were dissatisfied with their jobs but didn't know what job or career they wanted to pursue. If this describes you, know that you are not alone.

If you want to make a career move but do not know what move you would like to make, consider the desire to change as your starting point. Take some time to consider what you enjoy about your current job. Maybe you enjoy teaching but prefer teaching adults rather than young children or teenagers. Do you prefer coworkers who are friendly and outgoing, or would you rather work with coworkers who are focused more on work responsibilities and less on socializing?

I recently spoke with an elementary school principal who suggested that a teacher thinking about leaving the profession consider working at a different school before pursuing a new career. She has worked at several schools and explained that every school has a unique environment. She believes that a teacher unhappy in one environment may find job satisfaction at another school.

You may also benefit from reading *What Color is Your Parachute, A Practical Manual for Job-Hunters and Career-Changers*. This book in-

Consider

Reflect and think

deeply about

what you enjoy

and want.

cludes a self-inventory that will help you assess who you are and what you love to do. The author also provides information on selecting a career, securing a job, and starting your own business, if you choose to do so. This book has been published every year since 1970. Make sure that you obtain a recent edition, as the job market has changed significantly since the initial publication of the book.

QUESTIONS

1 What are five aspects of your present job that you enjoy? (Consider job responsibilities, work location, relationships with coworkers and supervisors, etc.)

2 What, if anything, would you change about your current job duties or work environment?

3 What activities do you enjoy doing that are not part of your current job?

Career Moves for Teachers and Other Professionals

Think about it.

After evaluating your current job, you may find that you want to continue working for the same employer but transfer to a different location. You may want to stay where you are but perform different responsibilities. If you're ready for a career move, prepare to move forward, but first consider what is bound to happen next, especially if you are contemplating a major change.

> "Fear kills
>
> more dreams
>
> than failure
>
> ever will."
>
> Unknown

Chapter Three
FEAR

Fear can be a paralyzing emotion.

We briefly considered fear in discussing change. Now we will address how to deal with it. First let's consider what it is that we fear. Of all the concerns associated with fear, three stand out as the most prevalent. First, the fear of criticism: "What will people say about me if I fail?" Next is the fear of discomfort: "What if achieving this goal requires a lot of time and energy?" Finally, and perhaps the greatest fear we may face when considering a career move, is fear of poverty: "What if I am unable to find a job or make enough money to support myself and my family with this new endeavor?"

Fear of CRITICISM

Shortly after I decided to go to law school, I attended a social event with several teachers in attendance. I overheard a teacher talking about a coworker, whom I will call Maggie. Maggie took time off from work to pursue a PhD; however, she discontinued her efforts prior to reaching her goal. The teacher sharing this information informed her listeners that although

Maggie was telling everyone that she dropped out of school because she missed teaching, the real story was that this poor soul was failing in her pursuit to further her education; thus, she had no choice but to abandon her hopes of receiving a doctoral degree. While listening to this information and how it was presented, several people laughed at Maggie's fate. I felt sick to my stomach, because I realized that if I failed in my attempts at furthering my education, people would talk negatively about me and laugh at my misfortune. The anticipated criticism that I could expect to receive if I failed induced symptoms of embarrassment and shame before I registered for my first course.

As a child my friends and I would often say, "Sticks and stones may break my bones, but words will never hurt me." However, that saying wasn't true when we were young, and it's not true now. Words can and do hurt. A career move, especially one that requires you to complete college courses, will include some risk of failure, and there are people who may talk negatively about you if you fail. However, there are also people who will say hurtful things even when you succeed.

It's been said that the unhappiest people in the

"As a child my friends and I would often say, 'Sticks and stones may break my bones, but words will never HURT me.' However, that saying wasn't true when we were young, and it's not true now. Words can and do hurt."

world are those that care the most about what other people think. The people I know who often talk about the failures of others are those who fear failure the most. Don't allow the fears of others to control your destiny. As difficult as it may be, accept the fact that people may say negative things about you. This may cause emotional pain or discomfort, but continue with your goal, taking that uncomfortable feeling in the pit of your stomach with you. Eventually, the emotional anguish will diminish.

Fear of DISCOMFORT

Not only did attending law school elicit the fear of failure, I knew it would require a tremendous amount of work to complete the required courses. I thought back to my first year as an elementary school teacher. I remembered staying up late at night and working weekends preparing lessons and activities. I thought law school would be worse, and it was.

Each decision to further my education or make a major career move was followed by a period of longer work hours, less sleep, and time spent working on activities and projects that I did not always enjoy. However, the difficult and uncomfortable times did not last forever. If you decide to change jobs, pursue a new career, or further your education, there may be times when you are uncomfortable. You may have to work long hours, at night, and on weekends. Chances are you faced discomfort in the past and pushed through difficult times. You've done it before. You can do it again.

Fear of POVERTY

Not having enough money to meet our financial obligations is not a fear to be taken lightly. An attorney once told me that she preferred staying in a job that she hated because she needed the money. She had experienced many stressful times in her life and stated that the worst stress of all was not having enough money to meet her financial obligations.

Staying in a job we hate is no guarantee of job security. I personally know individuals who were fired from jobs that seemed secure. Many of us know or have heard of individuals who worked in jobs deemed secure but were laid off during a period of "downsizing." If you have not done so already, start saving for a rainy day, as many of our parents advised. Remember also to handle credit responsibly so that it is available if needed.

When I decided to attend law school, I thought

I could attend school part time and work part time. However, part-time attendance was not an option. I was also advised not to work my first year. Though I was initially against incurring the debt of a student loan, I borrowed money at a low interest rate and repaid the debt as soon as possible. It was among the most profitable career investments that I ever made.

If it's time for you to make a career move, research your options. Start by looking for another job that allows you to use your training and skills to perform responsibilities that you enjoy. If you want to pursue a job or a career that requires you to further your education, visit a local college or university and talk with someone about the financial obligation and available financial assistance, if needed. Do not assume that you cannot afford to continue your education without researching the possibility.

Fear is normal. However, it doesn't have to prevent you from making a desired career move.

In *Think and Grow Rich*, Napoleon Hill explains that fears are nothing more than states of mind. He instructs his readers that one's state of mind is subject to control and direction.[7]

Possibility

Consider what

can be done.

Then figure out

how to do it.

Even if you cannot control your fear, do not allow it to control you. Accept the fear and continue to pursue your career goal. Even if you fail at your initial efforts, you can learn from the experience, make necessary adjustments, or amend your goal. You may also consider the worst that could happen if you attempted a career move and failed. More likely than not, the worst that could happen may be uncomfortable, but not fatal. Decide to accept the worst, then take the necessary steps to prevent the worst from happening.

QUESTIONS

1 Do you have fears about changing your current job or career? If so, what are they?

2 What are the worst things that could happen if your fears become a reality?

3 What steps can you take to reduce the consequences that will result from the worst things happening?

Career Moves for Teachers and Other Professionals

Think about it.

Giving in to fear may cause you to remain in a job or career even though you know that it is time to make a move. However, our next topic, complacency, is more catastrophic than fear. Why? Because we may not recognize that we are in the depths of this condition and suffering from its harmful consequences.

> "The tragedy of life is not found in failure but complacency. Not in you doing too much but doing too little. Not in you living above your means, but below your capacity. It's not failure but aiming too low, that is life's greatest tragedy."
>
> Benjamin E. Mays

Chapter Four
Complacency:
A SILENT KILLER

I heard that if you put a frog in warm water and gradually increase the temperature, the frog will boil to death, even if, at some point, it can jump out.

What if you are the frog? You may find yourself in a job that is slowly killing you. If you were to step back and see the danger for what it is, you could escape and avoid tragedy. But from the inside, the heat isn't quite enough to make you take that leap—until it's too late.

Merriam-Webster defines complacency as "self-satisfaction especially when accompanied by unawareness of actual dangers or deficiencies."[8] I believe complacency is a greater hindrance to career success than fear, because fear is recognizable, while complacency may go unnoticed. Even when you refuse to admit that you are afraid, you still have that feeling in the pit of your stomach when you face a challenging situation.

Signs of complacency may be invisible, especially to the person suffering from this malady. We may notice the symptoms in the nonchalant attitude of the cashier ringing up our groceries or in a coworker who arrives late, leaves early, and gives a mediocre performance in completing tasks. However, we may not see symptoms of complacency in ourselves. Ask yourself at the start of your next work week, "Am I doing work that I love?" You may say, "It's okay." You may yell, "No!" You may even start to cry. Any of these responses may be signs of complacency. A complacent attitude regarding your work may lead to poor performance, which can then lead to a demotion or termination.

At the start of my teaching career, I was energetic, had fun, and always looked forward to going to work. However, at some point I lost my zeal. At first, I couldn't even consider giving up teaching. I had a bachelor's degree and master's degree in education, along with years of experience. I never thought that I'd see the day I no longer wanted to teach. However, that day came, and I went on to pursue a new career. So can you.

> *"Signs of COMPLACENCY may be invisible, especially to the person SUFFERING from this malady."*

Action

Habitually and energetically moving in a positive direction.

QUESTIONS

1 Do you look forward to starting work most days?

2 If you had an opportunity to change jobs, or to change your career, would you?

3 Have you considered a job change in the past, but decided that it would be easier to continue working in your current job?

Think about it.

You realize that it is time for a job change or career move. You have faced your fears and are not deterred by them. You're not tempted by the comfort of complacency. You're now ready to set a goal, create a plan, and take action.

> "Setting goals is the first step in turning the invisible into the visible."
>
> Tony Robbins

Chapter Five
Set GOALS

If you're considering a significant career move, it may initially seem more like a wish than a goal. Start by setting a specific goal.

For now, don't worry about how you will reach that goal. We will get to that later.

Making a career move is like taking a road trip. It's impossible to start the journey if you have no idea where you're going. A specific goal lets you know where to go. Once you decide on the destination, you can decide what route to take in order to get there. If there's an accident or road construction on the route, you make a detour, then continue toward your predetermined location. When you know where you're going, it's easier to keep moving forward, even when you experience momentary setbacks. When you do not have a clear goal, you may be easily distracted and give up before making a concerted effort to get what you want.

The more specific your goal, the more useful it will be. During my first semester of law school

I decided that I would do something in education law. That goal was vague. However, when I decided to become a trial attorney litigating criminal cases within three months after graduating from law school, I could see my goal. It was also consistent with the goal I had in mind when I initially decided to become an attorney. The ability to see myself in a specific job kept me focused on completing courses and the required post–law school exams.

Similarly, a goal to become a principal of an elementary school in Miami-Dade County within the next five years is more specific than a goal to secure employment in a leadership position. Setting a specific goal to reach by a specific time increases the probability of reaching that goal.

Having a goal also helps us to set priorities. I started writing this book when I was still working full time on a job that was very demanding of my time. I dedicated several hours to writing on weekends. I am a member of a local Toastmasters club. (Toastmasters is an international organization designed to help its members develop speaking and leadership skills.) On a weekend that I had committed to working on a section of this book, I was asked

"Setting a specific GOAL to reach by a SPECIFIC TIME increases the probability of reaching that goal."

"I said no without any GUILT, because I had a specific goal that I was attempting to ACCOMPLISH."

to volunteer to help with a local Toastmasters' speech contest. It seemed to many people, including my husband, who is also a member of the organization, that a few hours on a Saturday could easily fit into my schedule. However, I knew that I would not reach my writing goal and keep up with my work responsibilities if I volunteered to help with the contest on the day that I was asked to do so. I respectfully declined to serve as a volunteer. I said no without any guilt, because I had a specific goal that I was attempting to accomplish. This brings me to another important reason why setting goals is so important.

Setting goals helps us to say no when the plans of others threaten to prevent us from reaching our goals. I like helping others, and when I see something that needs to be done, I have no problem taking on additional responsibilities at home, at work, or in social organizations. However, there have been times when I delayed work assignments and neglected completing my personal goals because I spent time helping others reach theirs. I've learned over the years that when I am not focused on completing my own plans, I find myself working on the plans of others.

If you are ready for a career move, but have not set a specific goal, I recommend that you spend time reading books and articles written to assist individuals seeking to find jobs or careers that are best for them. One previously mentioned is *What Color is Your Parachute? A Practical Manual for Job-Hunters and Career-Changers* by Richard N. Bolles. An internet search will reveal many others.

Although having a goal will keep you focused, your goal may change over time. While taking the steps necessary to reach your goal, you will receive new information, not only about your new career goal, but also about yourself. If, in the process of striving to reach a goal, you realize that the initial goal requires modification, know that it is not set in stone. Be flexible. Set a new or modified goal and focus on it.

This is perhaps a good place to note that I am primarily addressing career goals. A career is only one aspect of our lives. The ultimate goals for my life are to have peace of mind; to live a life that is physically, emotionally, and spiritually balanced; and to help others to do the same. Having a job that I enjoy is crucial to developing and maintaining the overall goals that I have set for my life. I am constantly growing

Focus

Clear and precise

vision of what

you desire to

accomplish.

and changing, and so are you. Therefore, a job or career that was a good fit at one time in your life may not be a permanent good fit. Don't be afraid to set a goal that seems best for you at this time. If needed, you can set a new goal in the future.

QUESTIONS

1 What is the job that you are seeking, or career move that you're ready to make?

2 If you haven't selected a definite goal, what books and/or articles will you read? Who will you talk with to help you set a new career goal?

3 If you haven't selected a definite career goal, when will you read the first book or article that will assist you? When will you schedule your first meeting with someone who can assist you with setting your new career goal?

Career Moves for Teachers and Other Professionals

Think about it.

After you decide what you want to do and you set a specific goal, you are now ready to create a plan.

> "A goal without a plan is just a wish."
> — Antoine de Saint-Exupéry

Chapter Six
Create a PLAN

A good place to start in creating a plan is to find people who have done what you want to do and learn how they did it.

Read books and articles about the career move you intend to make. Additionally, seek the advice of people you trust who can help you with creating and implementing your plan.

Although I previously advised against talking with everyone you know about your goal, there are people you should talk with as you begin creating your plan. These are individuals who have done or are doing what you have decided to do. They can provide insight on what you should do, when you should do it, and how it should be done. The information they provide may help you to avoid certain mistakes and pitfalls that you have no way of knowing about at the onset. Seek out someone who is working in a job or career that you are planning to pursue. Schedule a specific meeting time and be prepared to ask specific questions.

In addition to talking with someone personally, read books and articles written about the career that is of interest to you. There is an enormous amount of information available about most careers. Because you have selected a specific job or career, you can narrow your search so that your time is spent obtaining only the information needed to prepare your plan.

Keep in mind that there are individuals who may not have information related to your specific career goal, but who can assist you creating a plan. A career coach can assist with looking at your goal in a way you haven't yet considered. A representative at your bank may provide financial information, and your accountant can provide tax information. This is particularly important if your plan includes starting a business.

As previously mentioned, I decided to retire and start a mediation practice. As a mediator, I help parties resolve disputes prior to taking a case before a judge. After making the decision to retire and start a mediation practice, I talked with mediators who were mediating the types of cases I intended to mediate. I also shadowed other mediators and watched how they worked. I read books and articles on mediation

Coach

Someone to assist with reaching your goal.

and conducted online research for information on how to develop a mediation practice. I worked with a business development coach to help with planning, starting, and building a business. I talked with bank representatives, a financial advisor, and my accountant. I received valuable information, most of which I'd never considered. As I gathered information, I developed and modified my plan.

It may seem overly simplistic to suggest that you create a written plan. However, I have friends who have talked about goals and how they intended to reach those goals for years without ever taking the first step. A written plan keeps you focused on your major goal and can accelerate your achievement. However, your plan does not have to be elaborate. If you're seeking to change jobs within your current profession, or to make a career move that does not require you to make major life changes, simple to-do lists reviewed and modified regularly may be sufficient.

I'm a fan of to-do lists. Even when I decided to start a business, the process started with a list of specific things that I needed to do. After a while, I purchased a notebook to help organize my plan and stay on track. I have a major

> *"A WRITTEN plan keeps you focused on your major goal and can ACCELERATE your achievement."*

goal, with smaller goals and tasks that I need to complete in order to reach each small goal. My system is not perfect, but having everything in writing keeps me focused and on track. Find a system that works for you and make modifications as needed.

Our career goals may be totally different. But a written plan, reviewed daily, will keep your goal in front of you and increase the probability that you'll reach it.

QUESTIONS

1 Who is doing what you would like to do? Make a list.

2 When will you contact at least one person on that list?

3 Write your major career goal in a notebook. What are the specific tasks you need to complete to reach your new career goal?

Career Moves for Teachers and Other Professionals

Think about it.

After you set your goals and develop your written plans, it's time to make your goal a reality.

> "The path to success is to take massive, determined actions."
>
> Tony Robbins

Chapter Seven
Take ACTION

After setting your career goal and creating a written plan, it's time to take action.

Once you begin implementing your plan, you will receive additional information and feedback that may cause you to modify your plan or change it completely. Your original goal may also change. The sooner you take action, the sooner you'll achieve your goal or a modified goal that may prove to be better than anything you can possibly imagine at this time.

Author James Clear advises, "You do not rise to the level of your goals. You fall to the level of your systems."[9] Clear explains that goals are the results you want to achieve. Systems are the processes that lead to those results. I interpret systems to mean organized actions required to reach a goal. Although Clear suggests that we forget about goals and focus on systems, when it comes to focusing on your career goals, both are equally important. However, if you do not take the required action, having a goal is useless.

You may feel that the time is not right for you to initiate a major career change. The time is always right to set a goal and create a plan. You are not likely to set a goal today, create a plan today, take action today, and reach your major career goal today. When I registered for the Law School Admissions Test in my mid-thirties, I had no idea how I could afford law school or how I could possibly meet the curriculum demands required to receive a law degree. However, I created an initial plan based on what I knew at that time, and though the time was not yet right, I took action.

Setting and reaching new career goals is a process that takes time. So even if you are waiting for your children to finish school or for your life to get less hectic, start the process now. Accepting the excuse that the time is not right will only lead to failure and regret.

Author Jack Canfield advises, "Oftentimes, success happens when you just lean into it—when you make yourself open to opportunities and are willing to do what it takes to pursue it further. . . . You just start. . . . You see what it feels like. And . . . find out if you want to keep going—instead of sitting on the sidelines deliberating, reflecting, and contemplating."[10]

"The TIME is always RIGHT to set a goal and create a plan."

Several suggestions may assist you in successfully implementing your plan. First, consider getting an accountability partner—someone you can trust to hold you accountable for following through on your plan. This person should be someone who will consistently encourage you to continually take action toward reaching your career goal.

Next, review your plans regularly to make sure that you're on track. Depending on your plans, this may be a daily review. However, if your plans require you to receive a college degree or take classes to receive a certification, then once the course work is scheduled and initiated, your goals, at least those pertaining to your career, may not change daily or weekly; instead, you'll set smaller goals to stay on track with the requirements of your coursework.

If your goal is to change jobs with your current employer or to work in the same career, but with a different employer, you may have a goal of contacting several people each day who can provide guidance in helping you to secure a new position. The people you talk with may provide additional action steps that you will need to take in order to obtain a new job in your chosen career.

Accountability

Accept

responsibility for

reaching your

desired goal.

Although your goals and plans may be in writing, they're not etched in stone. Be willing to modify your plans as needed and continue to move toward reaching your goal.

QUESTIONS

1. What is the first or next step you will take in reaching your new career goal?

2. When will you take that step?

3. Name at least one person who will serve as an accountability partner. When will you contact this person?

Career Moves for Teachers and Other Professionals

Think about it.

If you need to make a career move and you know it's time to do so, take action now. You may not complete the plan and reach the desired goal immediately.
But the sooner you take action, the sooner you will reach your goal. However, before you begin your journey, make sure that you're prepared for any unforeseen obstacles that can disrupt your progress at any point along the way.

"I have learned that success is to be measured not so much by the position that one has reached in life as by the obstacles which he has had to overcome while trying to succeed."

Booker T. Washington

Chapter Eight
Unforeseen OBSTACLES

Chances are you will face obstacles at some point during the implementation of your plans.

It may be something small, like a fender-bender that requires you to put the cost of repairs on a credit card, creating unexpected debt. Or it may be something more devastating.

At the end of my first year in law school I faced an obstacle that seemed insurmountable at the time. I had been up all night studying and had just gotten into bed around three in the morning when the phone rang. It was my oldest brother. With as much composure as he could muster, which wasn't much, he informed me that my father had died suddenly of a massive heart attack. I had just talked with my father the night before about his plans for retirement. My parents had been married for almost fifty years. I couldn't imagine what my mother was going to do.

A few hours later, I was on a plane traveling from Gainesville, Florida, to Montgomery, Alabama. I don't remember how I got from Montgomery to Tuskegee, the town where my parents lived. After my father's funeral, I returned to school to take final exams. Preparing for and taking finals felt like climbing Mount Everest through pockets of quicksand. At times, I felt I was losing my mind and that I would never feel normal again. Friends, family, and my religious beliefs helped me through this most difficult time.

Before initiating a major change in your life, assess your support system. Whether it's a strong network of friends, spiritual beliefs, or a close-knit family, you will need help to stay grounded and continue the pursuit of your goals if the unexpected happens. If you do not have a support system, take it upon yourself to build one before embarking on your new venture; you will rely on it more than you might expect, even if everything goes as planned.

Few situations are more difficult than the death of a loved one during a moment in life that is already extremely stressful. Hopefully, you will not face such a challenge. But when you are living outside of your comfort zone and expe-

Geraldine Hogan

Support System

Family, friends, and spiritual beliefs that will help guide you through a difficult experience.

rience an unexpected tragedy, you can't allow that tragedy to prevent you from reaching your goals if you're physically and mentally capable of moving forward. I encourage you to be prepared—mentally, emotionally, and spiritually—to move through difficult situations so that you can get back on track, stay on track, and reach your goal.

QUESTIONS

1 Have you ever experienced a difficult situation that seemed impossible to overcome? How did you get through it? (If nothing comes to mind, think of something that seems minor now, but was a major problem when experienced.)

2 If a friend were faced with that same situation, what advice would you give?

3 Who would you call and what would you do if faced with an unexpected emergency today?

Career Moves for Teachers and Other Professionals

Think about it.

Unforeseen obstacles may be the most difficult to overcome because we do not know what will happen or when they will occur. Do not overlook the importance of having a support system in place. Even if you decide not to make a major career move, take the time to assess your support system. If you find that it is lacking, or nonexistent, strengthen or develop a network of family and friends, beliefs, or activities that you can rely on for strength and encouragement when faced with unexpected and tragic situations, should they occur.

A Few Last WORDS

Shortly before my retirement date, a colleague asked if I regretted my decision to retire. I immediately said no.

However, had he asked that question when I initially made this decision, he would have received a very different answer.

The moment my retirement decision was finalized, I began having second thoughts and mild panic attacks. I then reflected on a decision, made years ago, to end my career as an elementary school teacher. At the time it was impossible for me to see, with any form of certainty, the results of that decision. Yet, looking back over my legal career, I find that my journey has taken me to rewarding places and resulted in great personal growth, though the steps along the way were not always easy.

So again I ask, what about you? Do you need to make a career move? You probably know the answer to this question, whether you've invested a decade building your career, or only a few months or years. If it's time for you to make a move, don't allow fear or complacency prevent you from setting a goal, creating a plan, and taking action. Be prepared to address any unforeseen obstacles, should they occur. If needed, modify your plan or adjust your goal and continue the journey toward a successful career move.

> "If you can't fly,
>
> then RUN.
>
> If you can't run,
>
> then WALK.
>
> If you can't walk,
>
> then CRAWL,
>
> but by all means,
>
> KEEP MOVING."
>
> — Martin Luther King Jr.

About the
AUTHOR

Geraldine Hogan knows the triumphs and challenges, successes and defeats that accompany a decision to make a major career move. After working as a teacher for more than a decade, she stepped out of her comfort zone and pursued a legal career. After law school Geraldine moved from Gainesville, Florida, to Miami and began her legal career as a prosecutor for the Miami-Dade State Attorney's Office. She practiced workers' compensation law prior to receiving a gubernatorial appointment as a Judge of Compensation Claims for the State of Florida, in the Ft. Lauderdale District Office. In December 2018 she retired from her judicial position and with excitement and trepidation started a mediation practice, Geraldine Hogan, P.A.

Geraldine has a passion for helping others move beyond fear, complacency, and obstacles to decide what they want, create plans, and take the steps necessary to reach new career goals. To receive more information on how to make a career move, even if you do not know where to start, visit GeraldineHogan.com.

Learn more

If you enjoyed this book and would like to learn more from Geraldine Hogan, visit her website, GeraldineHogan.com for more about her workshops, courses, and speeches.

ACKNOWLEDGMENTS

To my brothers and sisters, Alverro, Linnie, John, and Nola. Thank you for your feedback and encouraging me to make this book a reality.

I am extremely grateful to Candace Duff for guiding me through the writing process and providing specific techniques that enabled me to complete this project. Thank you to Patrizia Sceppa for working on the interior design and to Layne Mitchelle for providing the cover design. Your talents enhanced the quality of this book and I am extremely grateful. Thank you, Liz Ferry, my editor. Your conscientious editing and perceptive suggestions were extremely valuable. Thanks to Paula Black for serving as a coach and a mentor and for helping everyone working on this project stay on track—from start to finish.

NOTES

[1] Norman Vincent Peale, *The Power of Positive Thinking* (New York: Simon & Schuster, 2003), 162.

[2] Johnnetta McSwain, *Rising Above the Scars* (Powder Springs, GA: Dream Wright, 2010).

[3] Jack Canfield, *The Success Principles: How to Get from Where You Are to Where You Want to Be* (New York: William Morrow, 2015), 229–30.

[4] E. Jones, *The People You Meet and the Books You Read* (Harrisburg, PA: Executive Books, 1985).

[5] Zig Ziglar, *See You at the Top*, (Gretna, LA: Pelican, 1977), 241–49.

[6] William Shakespeare, *Measure for Measure*, ed. Brian Gibbons (Cambridge Univ. Press, 2006) 1.4.77–79.

[7] Napoleon Hill, *Think and Grow Rich* (New York: Jeremy P. Tarcher, 2005), 263.

[8] Merriam-*Webster's Collegiate Dictionary*, 11th ed. (2014), s.v. "complacency."

[9] James Clear, *Atomic Habits: Tiny Changes, Remarkable Results* (New York: Penguin Random House, 2018), 27.

[10] Canfield, *Success Principles*, 143.

BIBLIOGRAPHY

Bolles, Richard N. *What Color is Your Parachute? A Practical Manual for Job-Hunters and Career-Changers*. New York: Ten Speed Press, 2019.

Canfield, Jack. *The Success Principles: How to Get from Where You Are to Where You Want to Be*. New York: William Morrow, 2015.

Carnegie, Dale. *How to Win Friends & Influence People*. Revised edition. New York: Simon & Schuster, 1981.

Hill, Napoleon. *Think and Grow Rich. Revised edition*. New York: Jeremy P. Tarcher, 2005.

McSwain, Johnnetta. *Rising Above the Scars*. Powder Springs, GA: Dream Wright, 2010.

Peale, Norman Vincent. *The Power of Positive Thinking*. New York: Simon & Schuster, 2003.

Ziglar, Zig. *See You at the Top*. 25th anniversary edition. Gretna, LA: Pelican, 2003.

So again I ask,

what about you?

Do you need to make

a career move?